JOYCE BANDA
Advocate for Women and Girls

Letitia deGraft Okyere

MACSWAIN PUBLISHING

Joyce Banda: Advocate for Women and Girls

Copyright © 2023 by Letitia deGraft Okyere

Illustrator: Artist Canvas
Layout designer: Nassim Sarkar

Library of Congress Control Number: 2023904221

All rights reserved.

No part of this publication may be reproduced, stored in a retrieval system, a database, and/or published in any form or by any means, electronic, mechanical, photocopying, recording, or otherwise, without the prior written permission of the publisher.

ISBN 978-1-956776-18-8 hardback
ISBN 978-1-956776-19-5 ebook

Published by MacSwain Publishing
editor@macswainpublishing.com

For
Gray John Mtila and Richard Banda
Joyce's destiny helpers

Acknowledgments

I wish to express my profound appreciation to those who have enabled me to embark on this book-writing endeavor. First, I thank God Almighty, for it is only in Him that I live, move, and exist. I owe Him a debt of praise I will never be able to repay. Second, I honor all the women who have had a positive influence on my life, giving me reassurance and guidance.

To my grandmother, who believed in me, and my mother, who saw something in me she called a talent when I had no idea what that word meant. To my mother-in-law, a source of encouragement. To my aunts. The one who gently corrected my grammar, another who gave me rides home from primary school in her Volkswagen Beetle, yet another who made delicious marmalades for my siblings and me. The aunt, who helped me understand how the hearing impaired appreciate music, and the other, who was my sister's godmother but never left me out. I remember the beautiful multicolored Ashia skirt and white blouse with lace trimmings she gave me. I wore it until it begged for mercy. Then my mother consoled me with my sister's, which she had outgrown, that sought mercy too. There is the aunt who gave me my first real job at the HM Inland Revenue, as it was known then. To the many more aunts I cannot mention.

To my sister and many sister-cousins; you stand by me no matter what. To my girlfriends who support me in diverse ways, some of whom are the first to sample my draft scripts, providing me with fair and critical reviews. To my nieces. The one who directs me to stretch regularly to maintain my posture as I age, and another who screams "Auntie Tish" in the background when she hears me talking to her mom on the telephone. The other who tells me outlandish stories to make me laugh and enjoys elevating her "level" in my life from niece to sister and to many more nieces.

To you fabulous women, may my appreciation for you rise to God Almighty as a sweet-smelling incense, causing Him to remember you. For those of you who have transitioned to the immortal, may the angels of God whisper to you my most heartfelt love and thanks. You all make my world go round.

To Her Excellency Mrs. Joyce Banda, for living such a life of inspiration, which provided me with the material to curate this book, *Joyce Banda: Advocate for Women and Girls*. May your light continue to so shine that those who see it may give glory to our Father who is in heaven.

I remain grateful.

-L.D.O.

**If we want to change Africa's narrative,
we need women leaders.**

Her Excellency Mrs. Joyce Banda
Former President of Malawi

Contents

Chapter I: The Name Joyce 1

Chapter II: The First Lesson 5

Chapter III: The Value of Learning 9

Chapter IV: Joyce Begins to Dream 13

Chapter V: Weekends at Malemia 17

Chapter VI: Awakening in Nairobi 21

Chapter VII: Life with Richard Banda 27

Chapter VIII: Building a Network of Businesswomen 31

Chapter IX: The Joyce Banda Foundation 37

Chapter X: Early Political Career 43

Chapter XI: The Journey to Kamuzu Palace 49

Chapter XII: Presidential Initiatives 59

Chapter XIII: Life After Politics 69

Chapter XIV: The Joyce Effect 75

Appendix A: Joyce's Leadership Nuggets 81

Appendix B: Accolades 83

Appendix C: Awards 85

Appendix D: References 89

The seeds of success in every nation on Earth are best planted in women and children.

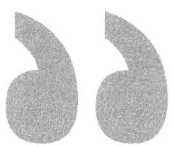

The Name Joyce

Everyone is born with a destiny, but not everyone uncovers it, never mind, walks in it. For Joyce Mtila Banda, born April 12, 1950, at the Domasi College of Education's clinic in what is now Malawi's Zomba District, her path was revealed early. This clinic, a few minutes drive south of Malemia, Joyce's hometown, set the stage for the first hint that her life would be driven by purpose. Malawi then was a British protectorate known as Nyasaland.

Joyce's parents, Gray John and Edith Chimwele Mtila, had high expectations for their baby daughter. For one thing, Gray and Edith were determined to do things differently. Customary beliefs preventing daughters from reaching their full potential as adults would be discarded. Gray and Edith made a commitment that any daughters they were blessed with would have as much value as sons. Therefore, this little girl would have the same opportunities as any boy in their community, even though traditional values favored boys over girls.

The first chance to abandon tradition occurred that very Wednesday, the day of Joyce's arrival. This was a decision not within the authority of Gray or Edith, but providence would have its way. Joyce was born into the matrilineal Yao tradition, which meant that she would be named after her maternal grandmother, Hilda. So, when Grandmother Hilda made her way to the clinic at Domasi, she expected to return home later that day, having confirmed Hilda as the new baby's name.

An excited Grandmother Hilda walked into the clinic and was directed by staff to the room where her daughter and her granddaughter rested. She took a glance at sleeping Edith and moved to the cot to pick up the baby for introductions. Just then, a British woman walked into the room and saw the baby nestled in her grandmother's arms. She was the healthcare professional who had established the clinic. Grandmother Hilda found out that she was a nurse with additional, specialized midwife training. The midwife asked the proud grandmother for the baby's name. Rather than respond Hilda as tradition demanded, Grandmother Hilda instead asked the midwife her name. She hesitated and gave Joyce. Grandmother Hilda wanted to know its meaning, and the midwife, with a gentle smile, said, "Joy." Grandmother Hilda nodded to herself; tradition would have to rest on the shelf this time. She named the newborn Joyce, pushing Hilda to second place. Taking on Joyce meant that the new baby lost out on being the next matriarch of the family. Grandmother Hilda was not bothered, she had seen the glimmer of a star. When Edith woke up after hearing voices, Grandmother Hilda told her about the change she made.

Grandmother Hilda would later explain to an older Joyce why she chose the name. She had been affected by the white nurse-midwife in her starched and primed uniform and desired that her granddaughter would grow up to carry a similar air of authority about her. In Grandmother Hilda's heart, Baby Joyce would become someone like Nurse Joyce, who helped women deliver new life into the world, bringing joy to many families. Thus, Gray and Edith's first daughter and child became Joyce Hilda Mtila, where hope, promise, and expectation overrode tradition.

In what way would Joyce Mtila follow in Nurse Joyce's footsteps? How would Joyce Mtila bring new life into being? How much joy would she bring to others? Grandmother Hilda just sensed a touch of her new granddaughter's destiny, having no idea where Joyce's authority would fall or how she would convey joy to others. The force of destiny would cause pieces of the puzzle to fall in place as Joyce grew.

An African woman carries heavy loads anyway. We are brought up that nothing is unbearable. I use that now, positively.

The First Lesson

After Joyce's destiny was revealed at her birth, it was reinforced by the nurturing she received at home and her life's journey. Joyce's first lesson came from being the eldest child in the Mtila home. By her tenth birthday, Joyce had learned responsibility; guiding and managing her siblings without parental supervision.

Joyce's father Gray was a policeman who became the first and most famous drum major of the police band. Edith, Joyce's mother, worked as a shop assistant at the Mandala Stores in Zomba. In those days in Nyasaland (now Malawi), it was rare to find mothers employed outside the home. Gray and Edith needed the extra income to place their children on a path to a secure future. As a result, Joyce, the eldest of what would be five siblings – a brother called MacArthur and sisters Festa Catherine, Cecilia, and Anjimile – became her mother's assistant by the age of seven years old, the leader of the Mtila children. Joyce was ten years old when Anjimile, the youngest of the girls was born. Joyce was so good at caring for MacArthur, Festa Catherine, Cecilia, and Anjimile, they called her Sister, not Joyce. It felt odd when they used her given name rather than Sister.

In the mornings, Joyce took MacArthur and Festa Catherine to school. In the afternoons, Joyce cooked, fed, and babysat all four of them, while she completed other household chores. Joyce kept Anjimile bouncing on her hip or strapped to her back. Sometimes, she had to carry Anjimile on her back as she played with friends from her school or neighborhood. When Anjimile felt too heavy or elder-sibling responsibilities weighed on her, Joyce placed Anjimile under a tree. There were moments when Joyce wanted to act like a normal little girl, with no care or concern. She never took her eyes off Anjimile as she played. Joyce surely did not tell her mother that she sat Anjimile under a tree while she spent time with friends.

When Joyce was eleven years old, Edith was admitted to hospital. Joyce ran the home as a little mother to her siblings. Now, she had even fewer breaks to study or play with her friends. While her younger brother had time to finish his homework and read books, Joyce had a long list of chores, checking tasks off as she completed each one. Gray was grateful as Joyce made it easier for him to leave for the police station in the mornings without too much worry about how the children would cope. When Edith returned home after her twelve months stay away, she was pleased by how well Joyce had managed the household. Life was preparing Joyce for a role of greater responsibility, with the home as her first class of instruction.

If we provide the young with a
strong foundation, we can leave behind
a legacy substantially greater than
most are able to bequeath.

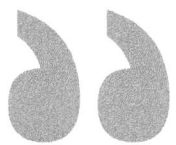

The Value of Learning

Joyce learned from her father the importance of being able to acquire new knowledge and skills, whether in a formal classroom or through other channels. Few girls were lucky to attend even primary school. When there was limited money available in a family, sons got the privilege of being educated while daughters stayed at home, cooking, cleaning, and fetching. Gray and Edith planned that Joyce and her sisters would have every chance to get an education, just as their son would. It did not matter that Gray's friends made fun of his efforts to educate Joyce. "What will you do with your educated daughter, Gray?" they asked him. Gray just ignored them.

Joyce got English grammar lessons from her father. She read a book daily and had to tell him about it. He made her listen to classical music, including those by Beethoven and Handel. Gray gave Joyce access to Jim Reeves and others, including Malawian music and his own compositions. Joyce's father taught her the difference between sound and noise and gave her voice training.

Many villages in the country have the *mphala*, a gathering place for men and boys to discuss social problems or simply to enjoy each other's company. Women and girls are not invited but Joyce still had mphala type conversations with her father. Gray spent time with Joyce and her siblings, debating issues of interest. Through Joyce's mphala talks, he taught her how to interact with adults and analyze matters of concern, whether to the family or community. Gray, unable to attend school as a child, insisted his children receive what he missed out on. Gray would not compromise on ensuring that Joyce reached her full potential.

One afternoon, Uncle John Kadzamira came to visit. Uncle John watched with interest as Joyce held a conversation with her father. As Uncle John prepared to return to his home, he told Gray that he sensed something different about Joyce, that she would become a national leader. Gray replied, "But John, she is only a little girl." "Well, this is what I know, and it carries weight. Don't ignore it, Gray," Uncle John said. Even though Gray laughed then, he often reminded Joyce what Uncle John had said. If Joyce remembered Uncle John's words, they would guide her choices for her future. Uncle John's vision of Joyce's potential strengthened Grandmother Hilda's hopes, although Joyce had no idea what it meant. Much like how Grandmother Hilda did not know exactly why she abandoned tradition to choose a name that spoke of promise for her granddaughter.

Gray and Edith's dedication to impart the value of learning pushed yet another piece of the puzzle into place. Also, because of her Gray's work as a policeman, Joyce was able to appreciate the different cultures across the country. Joyce's father was posted to different parts, and during her visits, she got glimpses of diverse traditions and beliefs. A necessary foundation for someone who would become a national leader, perhaps even a wedge in the puzzle. However, several more pieces would have to come together for Joyce to get an awareness of what the future held for her.

I am tremendously inspired by many women around the world who work under dire circumstances to make a difference for their families.

Joyce Begins to Dream

Chapter IV

Joyce's father believed role modeling was an essential part of encouraging Joyce and her siblings to develop their potential. Role models would make it possible for Joyce to dream of what she might become, the first step to achieving what might seem impossible. Joyce's contact with people who made a difference in their communities would help her embrace the aspirations that her parents, Grandmother Hilda, and Uncle John had for her, no matter how burdensome they seemed. Thus, Gray would create opportunities for Joyce to see what possibilities exist, with the force of destiny also playing its part.

When Joyce was around ten years old, for example, despite Edith's objections, Gray invited her to the Zomba State House, called the Government House at the time, for a concert by the police band. Gray was a member of the band. To Joyce's mother, it was inappropriate for Gray to take his young daughter to his place of work. The band was playing for Governor Sir Glyn Smallwood Jones and his wife. He softly explained to Edith that it was time for him to spark a different kind of flame in Joyce's heart. Joyce dressed up with excitement after Edith gave her approval. It was going to be just her and her father for this outing.

Joyce and her father left home with enough time for him to practice with the band. Joyce sat quietly in her seat, waiting for the event to begin. After it started, Joyce noticed that while the band and guests including herself remained in the gardens, the governor and his wife sat on the second-floor balcony. They were drinking tea as the band played. Joyce looked up at the balcony a few times, wondering how someone earned the privilege to sit there when everyone else stayed in the gardens below. Gray, never one to miss a teaching moment, said to her when she asked about it, "Joyce, you have the potential to go anywhere." Joyce was lost in her thoughts during the ride back home.

A few years later, an older Joyce went to the Zomba Plateau early some mornings to collect firewood used for the family's open stove. After Joyce and her friends walked back down the mountain with bundles of logs, they often rested under a large tree facing what is now the Old Parliament Building in Zomba, eating fruit they picked along the way. Joyce enjoyed watching members of parliament walk in and out of the building. This time, she noticed a woman dressed in a black and white suit, with white gloves and a hat. Joyce had never seen an African woman dressed so smartly in European clothing. When Joyce returned home, she asked her father about the woman she had seen going into the Parliament Building. She found out that the woman was Rose Lomathinda Chibambo, the first and only woman in Parliament. Joyce was captivated by Mrs. Chibambo's status in the national government. Again, she asked herself how a woman could rise high enough to sit in Parliament. Gray was pleased with this development because it showed that Joyce was beginning to dream.

Often, Joyce remembered Governor Jones sitting on the balcony or Mrs. Rose Chibambo striding into Malawi's new Parliament with confidence. These memories accompanied a replaying of her father's encouraging words. Yes, she was beginning to realize that she did have the potential to achieve whatever she set her mind to. But it was no good if Joyce only learned how to dream. She had to understand the relationship between hard work and achieving one's dreams. One way Gray did this was to invite people with advanced training to his home, to meet his children. They would generate Joyce's interest; her eyes lit up as she listened to these guests.

In addition, Joyce's home life gave her many chances to value the need for hard work. Joyce watched her mother Edith work outside the home to support Gray's income as a policeman. Grandmother operated a small-scale business in the village. Then there was Gray's life story, another example of how perseverance made dreams a reality. Gray's father died when he was eight years old, and his mother remarried a wealthy man who did not want a relationship with his two stepsons, Gray and brother Shaibu. Gray's mother and her second husband lived in

Zomba while Gray and Shaibu lived in the village. The two brothers walked about eight miles daily to school and back, past their mother's home she shared with her husband and three new younger siblings. When he was in the fourth grade, Gray was forced to drop out because there was no money for his tuition.

Gray did not give up. He joined the Nyasaland Police Band (later the Malawi Police Band) in the 1940s and taught himself music. Gray played the trombone at night events after a full day as a policeman. When he did not have a concert, he stayed up late studying. Joyce and her siblings went to bed many nights to melodious sounds from his trombone. Gray's efforts paid off, and he received a government scholarship in 1971 to study at the Royal Military School of Music in Britain. That same year, when the country's police force celebrated its fiftieth anniversary, Gray Mtila was honored with a thirty tambala (30 tambala or K0.30) stamp featuring a drum major. A tambala is the smallest unit of the Malawian currency, called the kwacha. On Gray's return home from Britain, he was employed by the exclusive Kamuzu Academy as one of the first African music teachers. Joyce appreciated her father's determination and the benefits it brought to the family. In 2000, ten years after Gray's death, he received the Millennium African Achievers Award and in 2011, the Malawi Order of National Achievers Award.

For Joyce now, more pieces of the puzzle fell in place. It was a good thing to dream but also important to value the process that made dreams possible. It would take another life changing event to fit a critical piece of the puzzle into place.

I was privileged because my father was
a policeman, and we lived in town.
Many people in Malawi are from typical
villages. My grandmother insisted I should
be in both worlds, and so I needed
to be acquainted with village life.

Weekends at Malemia

Chapter V

When Joyce was seven years old, she began to spend weekends with her maternal grandmother at Malemia, a town northeast of Zomba. The Yao tradition required Joyce, as the eldest daughter of the family, to be raised by her maternal grandmother. However, Gray and Edith asked that Joyce stay in Zomba, where she lived with her parents on weekdays and make the nine-mile bus ride to Malemia on Friday afternoons. There were better schools available in Zomba. Grandmother Hilda carried a lot of influence in the family as an elder member, but again, she was willing to depart from tradition to ensure Joyce got the best chance to fulfill her destiny. Gray may have thought that he skillfully persuaded Grandmother to allow Joyce to attend school in Zomba. Instead, Grandmother was determined that her granddaughter live up to her name and just smiled at Gray's earnest plea. She nodded enthusiastically at his short speech on why Joyce should remain in Zomba from Mondays to Fridays. Grandmother Hilda did not want to take the wind out of Gray's sails.

Grandmother had a list of chores for Joyce at Malemia. Joyce cleaned, carried heavy loads, and cooked over an open fire; a young girl must know how to maintain a home. Though weekends away with her grandmother did not put a break on housework, in Malemia, Joyce had no younger siblings to carry on her back or care for. From her grandmother, Joyce had additional opportunities to learn how to keep a home. Joyce also watched her grandmother's business activities and took notes on keeping accounts and managing operations. Grandmother's small-scale business employed several men and women. She earned enough to help Gray and Edith educate Joyce and her siblings. Grandmother worked hard for a living, and on weekends, Joyce assisted. Joyce enjoyed her visits with Grandmother.

In Malemia, Joyce met Chrissie, and they became inseparable, even though Chrissie was a year older. Joyce would get an awakening about her future path through this relationship with Chrissie. Every Friday after they became friends, when Joyce's bus arrived at her final stop, Chrissie would be there waiting for her. They talked non-stop, walking into the village together. Chrissie brought Joyce up-to-date on village gossip, and Joyce shared things that happened in Zomba. They played during the weekend when they both got breaks from household chores. Chrissie taught Joyce much about village life, picking wild fruits and vegetables, catching crabs, and swimming in the river. The girls often went to Zomba Mountain for mushrooms. The weekend always passed quickly for the two girls. Each Sunday evening, after Joyce and Chrissie parted, they began counting down until their next meeting. The girls could hardly wait for Fridays, and without fail, Chrissie would be at the bus stop to welcome Joyce back.

Joyce attended Zomba CCAP (Church of Central Africa Presbyterian) Primary, and Chrissie went to the local village school. Both girls were good students and earned places at two of the country's best secondary schools. Joyce went to Providence in Mulanje, about forty-six miles south of Zomba; Chrissie to St. Mary's in Zomba. After Joyce started at Providence Secondary, she went to Malemia for her visit and this time, Chrissie was not at the bus stop, and she was never coming back it seemed. Chrissie dropped out of St. Mary's during her first year because her family could not afford the tuition, while Joyce completed her secondary education. Chrissie went on to get married at fifteen years of age and her first child, born while she was fifteen years old, died. This saddened Joyce, pushing a critical piece of her future into place. Joyce vowed that when she grew up, she would send as many girls as possible to school. This, the start of what would be Joyce's lifelong quest for the rights of women and girls. This time, it was not Grandmother Hilda or Uncle John or Gray giving a voice or nudge to aspirations for Joyce; it went a step further, with Joyce beginning to accept her destiny.

I got married at twenty-two and remained in an abusive marriage for ten years. I made up my mind that it was never going to happen to me again. I made a brave step to walk out in a society where you didn't walk out of an abusive marriage.

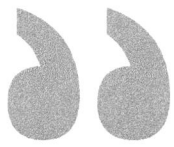

Awakening in Nairobi

Chapter VI

At the time Joyce completed secondary school, there were only a few places for higher education, and even these were not fully developed yet. She attended the University of Malawi to take a secretarial course, the only path allowed for women. Afterward, she did what was common for young women like her and sought employment. With a secondary school certificate and secretarial skills, there were decent openings available. At twenty-one years old, Joyce found her first job. A year later, Joyce married Roy Kachale and went on to have three children with him. Joyce soon recognized she was in an abusive marriage, but she did not have the courage to leave because divorce was not accepted in her society. Women were expected to stay in bad marriages; divorce was considered an embarrassment to the woman and her family. The belief was that once married, a woman had to quietly endure the difficulties associated with married life, including abuse of all kinds.

In 1975, Joyce moved to Nairobi, Kenya, to join Roy, who worked at Malawi's embassy. The physical and mental abuse did not stop. While in Kenya, Joyce heard about the women's rights movement influenced by leaders such as Jane Kiano, Nyiva Mwendwa, Julia Ojiambo, and Miriam Were. The activities by these women and other women's rights champions helped Joyce acknowledge that she was in an abusive relationship and to build the courage to think about ending the marriage. Joyce established a connection to the *Maendeleo ya Wanawake* (Women in Development) Organization, where Jane Kiano was the chairperson. Joyce realized that she had the choice to leave. In an interview many years later, Joyce said that before her exposure to the women's movement in Kenya, she did not even know "that as an African woman, you could begin to think about being equal to anybody."

When Joyce returned to Malawi, she separated from Roy, yet he continued to bully her and their children. One night he came to the home where she lived with her three children and threatened to kill all four of them. He banged on the door in anger and refused to leave. Joyce called her father, who had retired from the police as a sub-inspector. Gray contacted the nearest police station for assistance while Joyce woke up the children and eased them out through a back window so they could escape to a neighbor's home. She went through the back door as Roy tried to force himself into the home. She fell while escaping, ending up with a bleeding nose that did not keep her from running to the police station that her father had telephoned.

The police drove Joyce back to the house. By which time Roy had broken in and destroyed everything he laid his hands on. When the police discovered that Joyce was still legally married, their attitude changed. Joyce was informed that as officers, they could not interfere in a family matter. The police returned to the station leaving Joyce with no protection. Joyce got a taste of what it was like to have the rules operate against you. The next day, Joyce decided she did not care about the shame associated with divorce. She went to the courts to start divorce proceedings. In 1981, the divorce was finalized but she was destitute. A kind woman gave Joyce and her three children refuge for two years while Joyce pulled her life back together.

Joyce learned important lessons that would cause her to embrace her destiny as a champion for the rights of women and girls. The first lesson was how negative attitudes shaped women's and girls' acceptance of fewer opportunities because of their gender. The second was that women and girls must be taught how to achieve economic independence.

> They say endurance means a good wife, but most women endure abusive relationships because they are not empowered economically; they depend on their husbands.

Finally, laws needed to change in the drive for gender equality. Joyce's early adult life experiences taught her what high hurdles disadvantaged women must jump for a healthy and safe existence for themselves and their children.

The fire that would fuel Joyce's fight for equal rights for Malawian women and girls, and indeed all women and girls on the African continent, was lit. She was particularly concerned about girls because they received the least amount of attention and assistance to develop their potential. The little girl with a healthy foundation becomes the teenager who desires education or training to upgrade her life style. This teenager becomes the woman able to provide for her family and train her children to be valuable members of society. This same woman may become a local or national leader, serving as a role model with oversight for services or programs that benefit women and girls. Allowing girls who will become society's women to have access to similar advantages available to boys will greatly benefit communities and countries across generations. The final piece of the puzzle shaping Joyce's destiny snapped into place. Joyce now had a vision of her life's purpose as an advocate for the rights of women and girls.

My dear husband, Richard, has been the driving force behind my success and rise to whatever level I am now. My story and legacy are incomplete without his mention.

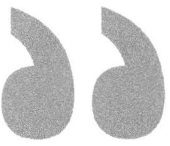

Life with Richard Banda

Though Joyce was free from her abusive relationship at age thirty-one years, she was handicapped, depending on the generosity of a kind elderly woman. Joyce knew she could not survive on a secretary's salary, and most importantly, that was not what she wanted to do with her life. Joyce built up her skills, attending an online institution to earn a bachelor's degree.

In the meanwhile, Joyce met High Court Judge Richard Banda. Many did not give their relationship a chance as they came from different tribes. The differences between these two tribes were so deeply rooted that members avoided intermarriage because it almost always ended in conflict. Marriage between those from the north and south of Malawi just did not happen. Even Edith, Joyce's mother, warned her that this choice would lead to another disaster and gave the marriage six months. But Joyce and Richard believed they had what it took to make it. In 1983, Joyce and Richard got married, and she found him to be a generous partner. As a member of the Malawian judiciary, Richard was better placed to help open doors in her journey to become an advocate for women and girls.

Richard adopted Joyce's three children, and with his four children, they began to build a life together as a blended family. Joyce and Richard adopted one more child and had two more daughters together. To keep her large and blended home of ten children, Joyce openly demonstrated affection and appreciation for Richard, loved all the children equally, and respected the biological mothers of her other children. Over the years, Joyce and Richard established traditions that nurtured a closeness. Joyce loved to cook for the family, and Richard presented a bouquet of flowers each Mother's Day, Valentine, and birthday to Joyce. They took a yearly two-week vacation at their home in Nkhata Bay. The family built a treasure trove of precious memories during these breaks when the boys got into all sorts of mischief. As the children grew, the family continued to find ways to spend time together, including driving hundreds of miles across the United States for a Christmas gathering when the older children were at university.

When Richard suffered a massive stroke in 2009, it put the family in a state of panic. At the time, he was serving as the Chief Justice of Eswatini (formerly known as Swaziland). He had retired as Chief Justice of Malawi in 2002 and received the Eswatini appointment a few years later. Richard lost his ability to walk and speak and could not remember the names of his wife or children. Joyce kept her faith in God, and Richard miraculously recovered, even though his doctors warned the family that such an outcome was impossible. Richard regained his ability to read, write, speak, and walk. He retired from his position in Eswatini, thinking it was time to live at a slower pace. However, Joyce would soon begin her ascent into high political office, a period that brought fresh challenges for the family and attacks on her life. It was just as well Richard was retired from his official appointment because he could then provide the support that Joyce needed.

> I convinced myself that economic empowerment of women was going to be key, especially in a country like this where most women didn't go to school.

Building a Network of Businesswomen

Joyce was now free to walk in her destiny. With Richard's backing, Joyce established and managed several businesses. Ndekani Garments opened in 1985 and within two years, it became the largest industrial garment manufacturing company owned by a woman in Malawi. There was also Akajuwe Enterprises, started in the early 1990s, and Kalindizga Bakery, in the mid-1990s. These businesses made Joyce more economically independent, and she realized just how important it was for women to gain financial freedom. During this season in her life, she worried about those women who were not as fortunate as she had been in finding the needed support to make a clean start. What happened to the woman who did not have the courage to leave an abusive marriage or the woman who did not have the financial resources to provide for herself and her children if she separated or divorced her husband? Joyce yearned to reach out to such women who had no refuge from the difficult life they lived. She pondered over how to meet this obvious need.

> Two years later I got married again, to my husband who was a high court judge in Malawi. For the next two to three years, I moved from zero to hero: I was running the largest business owned by a woman in Malawi in industrial garment manufacturing. But when I looked back, his [Richard's] fingerprint was all over it: if I wanted training, he paid; if I wanted a loan, he came [to the bank] with me. Because of his status in society, everything was easy for me. So, I had succeeded but I had succeeded because I was privileged. And that's when it began to worry me. I began to think about those that were in my past situation, but unable to walk out of an abusive marriage, or maybe those who did not know where to go, or those in a single-headed household, or widows. What could I do to reach out to them, I thought.

Joyce decided to use her successful business as a platform to promote financial independence for women. This would give women the confidence to leave abusive relationships and unhealthy environments. Joyce gave lectures to women on establishing businesses and managing operations. Soon, a group of women who were tomato farmers selling produce at the markets and on the streets graduated to opening their own shop using profits earned. This was an early indication that her sessions with women produced positive results. Now, Joyce wondered how she could increase the number of women who could benefit from this type of service.

In 1987, Joyce was one of two women invited to attend a meeting on how the Malawian government could partner with the private sector to grow the economy. This was a gathering organized by the United Nations Development Program. Joyce gave her opinion on the government's failure to rely on the private sector as a vehicle for national economic growth. At the event, Joyce met Don Henry, an official of the United States Agency for International Development (USAID), who offered his assistance in any way possible. The opening came through a USAID grant in 1989, allowing Joyce to tour the United States for six weeks, visiting organizations operated by women. Joyce heard about a nationwide group for businesswomen and planned to build a similar network of women in Malawi, to push for equal rights in business. She hoped to start with about one hundred women, support business ventures, and educate the government on laws and policies needed.

> I sat down in 1989 and I made up my mind at that point that I was going to spend the rest of my life assisting women and the youth to gain social and political empowerment through business and education.

On Joyce's return from the United States, she held discussions with friends, leaders at the Ministry of Women and Community Services, the Commission of Women in Development, and the Small Enterprise Development Organization. Don Henry put Joyce in touch with USAID's agent in Malawi who provided information on funding sources. The USAID paid for Joyce to study microfinancing in Bangladesh and India.

With a grant from USAID, Joyce created the non-governmental organization known as the National Association of Business Women (NABW) in Malawi around 1990. Joyce's message was simple, "This is our time." Within a few years, the NABW built a network of over thirty thousand women across the country. Women got access to business training, markets, and funding sources. The NABW promoted trade and the implementation of policies that included women in local and national decision-making. The network touched many lives, as a high proportion of women in the NABW were the primary income earners in their families.

The NABW was so successful that two years after its establishment, a group of husbands, annoyed by Joyce's impact on their wives, destroyed her garment factory. The factory had one hundred employees, but the irate men were not concerned about the loss of income for Joyce's staff. The men resented the independence their wives had achieved and took it out on Joyce. There was a lesson amid the chaos. Joyce knew she had to change her methods. Men must be encouraged to work alongside women.

> We need to know that for us [women] to succeed, we [women] need to work with and engage our men. Men are not our foes but, friends in the struggle.

Joyce was again reminded of the importance of both men and women collaborating for women's empowerment after she returned from the 1995 Fourth World Conference on Women held in Beijing, China. Joyce was inspired and immediately after her return home, began working to increase women's participation in national politics. At a Trade Fair Site event, Joyce organized the *Bringing Beijing Back to Malawi* initiative with the banner, *99 Women in Parliament by 1999*, as the objective. The men who passed by her table asked how she planned to achieve this; after all, there were men already holding these positions. She thought that if men had participated in the Beijing event, they would have gathered that it would take a unified effort by both men and women to improve women's rights. The men would not be aggrieved by what she was trying to achieve. Joyce learned that leaving men out of the discussion would not further the objective of increasing the number of women in leadership. In Africa, women were always central to state- or community-level leadership. In many ancient kingdoms, women committees selected the next ruler. Women lost their rank in leadership after colonization when these kingdoms were disbanded. The issue here is not whether women have the capacity to lead; history shows that they do. The challenge is including men in the quest for equal opportunities for women.

Around 1995, a group of women from Lunzu, a village ten miles from Blantyre, paid a visit to Joyce, then executive director of the NABW. The government had established a small lime factory for the village cooperative. The land belonged to the women because it was a matrilineal society, but the men controlled the cooperative and therefore, the income from the lime factory. The women pleaded with the men for a partnership and a share of the profits, but the men refused. The women turned to Joyce for a way to resolve differences with their husbands. The women saw no simple way forward. They either opposed their husbands with a likely negative bearing on their marriages or continued pleading for membership. Whichever way, the women were left without economic power.

Joyce remembered her lesson from the early 1990s when her garment factory was destroyed. She told the women from Lunzu that the best way would be for them to build their own factory. With time, the men would soften and become more willing to work together, and that was key. They laughed at the impossible dream. Joyce helped them form a cooperative of thirty-five women with funding from the European Union. They opened a small lime factory and received training to operate it. They got assistance with opening bank accounts which they signed with thumbprints. While all the preliminary activities for the women's cooperative were taking place, the men were not bothered because their factory was doing well and bringing in decent profits. The men tacitly gave their approval for the women to have their own factory.

However, months after the women's factory was fully operational, the men's factory broke down. The men set their eyes on the women's enterprise. They went to the women, trying to coerce the women to allow them to operate the new factory. The women insisted that funding conditions required that they managed the factory. When Joyce visited Lunzu with the United Nations Ambassador to formally open the new factory, she found the men employed by the

34 - Chapter VIII: Building a Network of Businesswomen

women, crushing stones in the mine in open heat while the women remained in the shade managing the plant and controlling the income. Working with the women of Lunzu, Joyce had found a way to get the men's cooperation without resistance.

During the 1990s, Joyce did not limit herself to the NABW. She was active on the international scene. She co-founded the African Federation of Women Entrepreneurs in 1993. It is a group advocating for businesswomen to participate in local, national, and international economic activities, now active in over forty countries in Africa. Joyce also had a hand in creating the Council for the Economic Empowerment of Women and the American and African Business Women's Alliance, serving as the first president of the latter. Both groups improve outcomes for women in business.

By 2000, a decade after its founding, the NABW had reached fifty thousand women across Malawi, easing the burden of poverty. NABW built partnerships with international organizations such as the Humanist Institute for Development Cooperation at The Hague, in the Netherlands, in 2003. The NABW demonstrated that financial independence would thrust women into leadership roles or representation at local or national levels. Today, the NABW still teaches women how to build and grow businesses while teaming up with policymakers to develop and implement regulations that advance women's business activities.

Under the Foundation, we have a huge program that targets women to teach them about HIV and other diseases and to give them economic empowerment.

The Joyce Banda Foundation

Chapter IX

Joyce thought of ways to fulfill the promise she made to send as many children to school as possible after she found out Chrissie could not continue with her secondary education. The NABW did not reach girls directly; neither did the Young Women's Network, another group she founded. Thus, Joyce decided to create an organization that addressed this gap, aimed at reaching girls. Before taking concrete steps toward this objective, Joyce obtained a diploma in non-governmental organizational management from the International Labor Organization's (ILO) training center in Turin, Italy. Joyce worked with the Hunger Project of New York, United States, to create the Malawi Hunger Project. The Malawi Hunger Project and NABW focused on hunger and poverty in rural households. Joyce had no idea this would be the channel by which her childhood ambition would come to life. In 1997, Joyce won the *Hunger Project Africa Prize for Leadership for the Sustainable End of Hunger* jointly with the President of Mozambique, Joaquim Chissano.

Joyce invested her prize money into establishing the Joyce Banda Foundation (JBF) to enhance the lives of girls and women. Joyce pushed the boundaries beyond the initial pledge of providing access to education, adding youth development, healthcare, leadership training, and income generation activities. The Foundation now focuses on children, youth, and women, operating through three main branches, the Orphan Care and Education Program, Market Women Activities Initiative, and Youth Movement in Development. Joyce's 2006 *International Award for the Health and Dignity of Women* from the United Nations Population Fund recognized her efforts in improving Malawian women's rights. By 2010, JBF had reached some 16,500 people, and in 2021, inaugurated the Community Development Initiative. JBF celebrated its twenty-fifth anniversary in 2022, launching five more projects covering post-graduate scholarships, industrial garment manufacturing, and boys' mentorship.

Joyce Banda Limited, a for-profit company, operates primary and secondary schools in Chimwankhunda, Blantyre. Joyce recruited two of her sons to operate the private institutions, growing enrollment from two hundred to one thousand in a few years. Profits from these private schools support the Orphan Care and Education Program. This branch of JBF provides education and nutrition to orphans and other needy children through its centers, numbered over thirty across Malawi. When operating at their maximum capacity, the centers feed up to ten thousand children daily and provide food packs for those with HIV/AIDS. A single center may distribute four hundred and fifty meals daily and deliver an early childhood curriculum to the children. The initiative has a free secondary school for orphans in Zomba. It has also assisted over 2,500 students with secondary, university, and technical school costs. For example, as of April 2022, the Foundation had sponsored thirty-two medical doctors. An important part of the curriculum is teaching boys and girls to respect each other and building girls' self-confidence. Joyce collaborates with Chrissie to identify girls who would benefit from the free tuition program. The childhood bond between Joyce and Chrissie was revived through JBF's work. The two friends travel together to meetings beyond Malawi to speak on women and girls' rights to education.

JBF became so well-known that little girls sought Joyce's attention for access to its benefits. A little girl who was regularly abused by her father gathered courage to let her mother know. After her mother questioned her father, he got angry and refused to pay his daughter's tuition. This little girl enjoyed going to school and the safety net the environment provided. Refusing to give up, she heard about JBF and searched for an avenue to meet Joyce. She told Joyce her story and received support to remain in school. In addition, Joyce encouraged the mother to tell her story on television, and the little girl's father was arrested and charged with physical abuse of his daughter, removing him from the home. JBF helped create conditions for the girl at her home and school where she could thrive.

The second program JBF operates is the Market Women Activities Initiative (MWAI). Joyce's inspiration came from a similar group established by former President of Liberia Ellen Johnson Sirleaf. JBF's MWAI is a network for market women. It assists women with establishing businesses, provides management training, supports village banking through small loans at low-interest rates, and enables business setup with donations of seeds, goats, and poultry for farmers. MWAI members are identified by its signature bright green cloth, designed by one of Joyce's elder daughters for its launch. MWAI has a membership of 400,000 rural women across Malawi, with five thousand involved in chili and soya bean farming. It has partnered with Telekom Networks Malawi, a telecommunications company, to give women access to digital banking through the distribution of mobile telephones. This digital banking aspect has grown to include men. Women also gained the capacity to operate their own booths selling Telekom Networks Malawi products.

The third program, Youth Movement in Development (YOMODE) trains the youth to contribute to their communities. For example, YOMODE provides carpentry classes where youth assist with the construction of shelters for the elderly and coffins for burials. YOMODE's seed and fertilizer subsidies support youth farmers.

JBF's 2021 Community Development Initiative sought to improve rural living in Malawi with the construction of modern villages. These villages will have electricity, modern housing, with a school, clinic, and community center, and an agricultural business foundation to ensure food and nutrition security. The Community Development Initiative and its partners plan to construct 1,400 houses in seven districts during its first phase. In April 2022, the foundation stone was laid for the rural clinic in Kasungu, one of the seven districts.

JBF is a grassroots organization focused on the economic empowerment of girls, youth, and women, and allows men to benefit directly from some of its initiatives. The Foundation has constructed clinics in four of the two hundred villages where it operates. It has collaborated with groups such as the Jack Brewer Foundation, which tackles poverty and other human rights issues in Africa and other parts of the world. JBF has grown over the years and now has an international presence with offices in South Africa and the United States.

> **My vision is a Malawi where men and women live in peace and harmony as equals enjoying their human rights.**

Early Political Career

Joyce's first brush with the political scene occurred in 1987 after her garment industry grew, and she had built a reputation as an activist for women's and girls' affairs. Hastings Kamuzu Banda, Malawi's first president, appointed Joyce to three national-level boards, expanding electricity supply, assisting rural traders, and strengthening services for disabled persons. These board roles were all linked to her desire to eradicate challenges faced by Malawian women and girls in rural areas. President Bakili Muluzi succeeded Hastings Kamuzu Banda and recognized Joyce's contribution as a board member of the Electricity Supply Corporation of Malawi, Development of Malawian Traders Trust, and Malawi Council for the Handicapped (MACOHA). President Bakili Muluzi promoted Joyce to board chairperson of three new institutions, the Malawi Housing Corporation, Agricultural Development and Marketing Corporation (more commonly known as ADMARC), and Malawi Communications Regulatory Authority (MACRA). Here, Joyce addressed housing issues, promoted agricultural exports, and monitored communication services.

These early appointments gave Joyce insight into government operations and allowed her to apply the knowledge gained as a private entrepreneur to public institutions. She brought a different and critical perspective to the process of building up public sector efficiency. Joyce also interacted with government officials frequently through her advocacy for gender equality but remained focused on seeking change as a private citizen. Thus, for years, she was content with lending her expertise in this fashion. As Joyce passed her fiftieth birthday, she reflected on her role as a women's and girls' champion, raising living standards. She began to see a place for greater impact, where she could influence the laws and policies that enabled practices affecting women and girls in a negative way. Perhaps the time had come for a different approach, particularly as her husband Richard had retired as Malawi's Chief Justice two years earlier, and her children were grown, requiring less daily supervision.

In the May 2004 general elections, Joyce stood as a parliamentary candidate for the Zomba Malosa constituency in the Zomba District. Joyce was encouraged by community members who had witnessed the bearing of her grassroots activism for women and girls. Joyce won the seat as a member of the United Democratic Front (U.D.F.), whose presidential candidate was Bingu wa Mutharika. Soon after taking the Zomba Malosa seat in the National Assembly, President Bingu wa Mutharika appointed Joyce as Minister for Gender, Child Welfare, and Community Services. Here, she could bring lasting change, the type she visualized when she decided to seek political office. Joyce tells the hilarious story of her first day at the ministry's office when she sat in the guest chair rather than at the minister's desk where she belonged. She had spent so many years dealing with the ministry as an outsider that she automatically went to the guest chair. Joyce uses the incident to underscore the need for humility, to live by a moral compass, combining knowledge with wisdom, and only doing that which is advantageous to those served.

Soon after her appointment to the Ministry of Gender, Child Welfare, and Community Services, Joyce received a call from the United States Ambassador to Malawi, who threatened to remove financial aid if Malawi did not tackle its child trafficking practices. An earlier paper had reported that thirty-seven percent of children between five to fifteen years old were child laborers, mainly working on tobacco and tea plantations. Joyce had wondered what the ambassador meant by child trafficking in Malawi. Joyce knew Malawi had a child labor problem and realized the ambassador referred to the link with child trafficking as children were being moved from home to plantations. Joyce initiated the National Platform for Action on Orphans and Vulnerable Children and the Zero Tolerance Campaign Against Child Abuse. These groups would identify ways in which children could be protected, change laws, expand access to education and healthcare, provide skills training, and penalize farms employing children. Joyce created the *Children's Corner* project, staffed with two child welfare officers for

each constituency. The officers received training and bicycles, introducing Children's Corners on Saturdays. The welfare officers invited community children to the assigned Children's Corner, where they were allowed to play with each other. This non-threatening method led to the collection of information on challenges faced by children in a particular community. If children felt comfortable with a welfare officer in the company of other children, they would be more likely to talk about problems they faced and seek assistance.

Joyce set her sights on the Prevention of Domestic Violence Bill, which had failed to pass for several years. Joyce knew from personal experience that laws and policies were a critical part of protecting women from domestic abuse. Passing the Domestic Violence Bill through Parliament was a huge task that she decided to tackle step by step. Joyce worked with leaders like Emma Kaliya from the Gender Coordination Network and other women's groups to draw attention to the need for the law. To get civil society's buy-in, she launched a media campaign to explain the problem and how it was resolved by the bill. She arranged for women to tell their domestic abuse stories on national television and radio, increasing awareness of the problem and its painful outcomes if not resolved. It changed attitudes. A woman did not have to accept domestic abuse and communities must not tolerate it. Joyce's fight for women's rights gained such attention she became known for the saying, "Don't abuse your wife; Joyce Banda is angry."

One day as Joyce drove into a village, she passed a man and wife walking along the way. The wife balanced a load of flour on her head while carrying a live chicken in one hand. The husband, who was dressed in a suit had removed his shoes which he passed to his wife to carry in her other hand because his feet hurt. Joyce stopped her vehicle next to the couple and asked the man to carry his own shoes. If he refused, she would take a picture of him and send it to the television station. He angrily asked Joyce to mind her own business. Another man riding a bicycle close by overheard the conversation and added, "Don't you know her, she is Joyce Banda." The man took his shoes from his wife and put them back on.

Joyce went to the leader of the largest opposition party in Parliament, arguing that it was a necessary change for the protection of women and children. With support from Oxfam and the United Nations Population Fund, Joyce held meetings with members of Parliament to discuss the bill and its importance. Joyce organized a march through the city and asked President Bingu wa Mutharika if the other two women in his Cabinet could join her. President Bingu wa Mutharika agreed and asked male Cabinet members to join as well. The Malawi Police Band made an appearance at the march, as did thousands of people. When the bill came to Parliament for a vote, it was nothing new to all parliamentarians, and it had President Bingu wa Mutharika and his Cabinet's endorsement. Joyce had one regret, though, that she had to remove clauses related to one type of domestic abuse. It caused her a great deal of frustration, but she had a choice to make, whether to let the bill fail again or accept this as an important victory in the process to end all types of domestic abuse. Joyce decided that this critical first opportunity must not be lost, and the Prevention of Domestic Violence Bill was passed in 2006. Unlike similar legislation passed in other countries, Malawi's addressed violence against both women and men.

After Joyce's success at the Ministry of Gender, Child Welfare, and Community Services, President Bingu wa Mutharika appointed her to Foreign Affairs as minister on June 1, 2006. This occurred even though she still belonged to the United Democratic Front while President Bingu wa Mutharika was a member of the Democratic Progressive Party (D.P.P.), founded by himself in 2005 after a dispute with the U.D.F. leadership. As Minister for Foreign Affairs, Joyce developed a relationship with the People's Republic of China. Through this renewed bond between the countries, Malawi's new Parliament Building in Lilongwe, designed by Malawian architects, was completed by a Chinese mining and construction company.

During this time, Joyce witnessed a change close to her heart. She had campaigned for years to have a street named after Mrs. Rose Chibambo. Malawi needed to acknowledge Rose Chibambo's contribution to the struggle for independence from British rule, and as Malawi's first woman member of Parliament and Cabinet minister in President Hastings Kamuzu Banda's government. Rose Chibambo was present in 2009 when President Bingu wa Mutharika finally honored her by naming a street in Mzuzu, in northern Malawi, after her. Three years later, Rose Chibambo's image was placed on the Malawi banknote for two hundred kwachas (K200).

Throughout my career, I have been confronted with people who have doubted my ability to achieve the dreams and ambitions distilled into my soul by my father.

The Journey to Kamuzu Palace

Chapter XI

During the 2009 general elections, Joyce ran as vice president with presidential candidate Bingu wa Mutharika under the Democratic Progressive Party (D.P.P.) umbrella. Bingu wa Mutharika faced a growing call for women to play a more significant part in national political decision-making. Thus, Joyce, with her background and reputation, was a natural choice as his running mate. Joyce had canceled her United Democratic Front (U.D.F.) membership and joined the D.P.P. earlier.

The D.P.P. won the elections and on May 29, 2009, Joyce was sworn in as the first woman Vice President of Malawi. President Bingu wa Mutharika gave Vice President Joyce Banda managing positions over national agencies, Non-Governmental Organizations (NGO), Disaster and Relief Administration, Safe Motherhood and Maternal Health, and HIV/AIDS. Joyce's popularity increased with a continuation of her work improving the living standards of women and girls. In 2010, she became a founding member of the Global Leaders Council for Reproductive Health, an organization of current and former heads of state and policymakers focused on increasing political will and financial backing for better reproductive health outcomes. Joyce was also a Goodwill Ambassador for the African Union Safe Motherhood program. Both roles added to her international presence.

As 2010 ended, though, Joyce's relationship with President Bingu wa Mutharika fell apart. President Bingu wa Mutharika wanted to install his younger brother, Peter Mutharika, Minister for Education, Science, and Technology, as his successor. Joyce disagreed with the action and expressed it; she would not accept Peter Mutharika as D.P.P.'s candidate for the 2014 general elections. The country was not a private business organization belonging to the Mutharika family. There were processes for selecting presidential candidates which must be followed. She argued that the fate of Malawi could not rest in the hands of one or two people. There was no room for a Mutharika family dynasty, as that would only spell disaster for the country.

With the country looking forward to the 2014 general elections, Joyce warned of a difficult time ahead. President Bingu wa Mutharika had lost the confidence of Malawians. His success with the agriculture program boosting food supplies was forgotten, overridden by his opulent displays of wealth. He had purchased a $13 million presidential jet and lived in a fifty-eight-room mansion while the majority of Malawians suffered severe economic hardship.

Joyce did not hesitate to voice her disapproval of government policies that made life more difficult for Malawians. President Bingu wa Mutharika also received negative press coverage from both national and international papers. His autocratic leadership style was criticized by leaders in countries that Malawi depended on for financial aid. This led to rumors that President Bingu wa Mutharika would be investigated for corruption by his successor. The likelihood of this happening increased if the successor happened to be someone like Joyce. On the other hand, if he paved the way for his brother Peter Mutharika, he would have certain protection from corruption charges. Therefore, Joyce's reputation had to be ruined because her position as Vice President of Malawi was a huge stumbling block to President Bingu wa Mutharika's plans for Peter Mutharika's succession. Many remembered that President Bingu wa Mutharika had hounded his predecessor, former President Bakili Muluzi, with arrests for charges that were later dropped for lack of corroboration. President Bingu wa Mutharika knew that, in his case, there was mounting evidence against him.

When it became clear that Joyce would stick to her convictions, President Bingu wa Mutharika tried to isolate her, putting pressure on D.P.P. colleagues not to associate with her. A D.P.P. member faced dismissal from the party for merely having meetings with Vice President Joyce Banda. President Bingu wa Mutharika and his followers launched an attack on Joyce's capabilities, hoping to put an end to the possibility that she might run in the 2014 elections as a presidential candidate. A D.P.P. official went as far as to tell a newspaper in 2010

that the country was not ready for a woman leader, making an indirect reference to Joyce's potential candidacy in 2014.

Joyce's support from Malawians did not waver during these difficult circumstances; rather, it grew within women groups and other entities. Emma Kaliya, the chairperson of the Gender Coordination Network, pointed out that women in Malawi were being treated like second-class citizens. The Malawi Public Affairs Committee, an important body of religious leaders, issued a statement in August 2010, asking President Bingu wa Mutharika to respect Vice President Joyce Banda's dignity. When in the same month, Joyce did not attend a D.P.P. governing council meeting due to the hostile treatment, members tried to pass a motion for her removal from the party leadership based on her absence. This failed because it could not be implemented retroactively. President Bingu wa Mutharika removed all Joyce's roles, including that of Goodwill Ambassador for the African Union Safe Motherhood program. Over the previous years, Joyce had become a much sought-after international conference speaker on women's and girls' rights and development. President Bingu wa Mutharika believed these international roles made Joyce a formidable opponent.

The D.P.P. tried to exert more pressure on Joyce to endorse Peter Mutharika as president for the 2014 general elections. That failed to change Joyce's mind, and she was stripped of several more roles. President Bingu wa Mutharika took over Joyce's positions at the Non-Governmental Organizations and Disaster and Relief Administration and handed over those at the Safe Motherhood and Maternal Health and HIV/AIDS programs to his wife, Callista. Callista stepped into the fray by describing Vice President Joyce Banda as a *mandasi* woman, i.e., a person of no consequence who had no right to think that she had the capacity to be president. Callista referred to Joyce's role and accomplishments through organizations such as the NABW and JBF. The fact that Joyce had worked previously with Callista Mutharika at the Hunger Project was no cause for restraint on Callista's part. Joyce turned the tables on Callista by embracing what was meant to be a demeaning label. Yes, she was a spokesperson for women in the lower income bracket trying to earn a living, desiring financial independence and the ability to provide for their children.

I am a mandasi woman, and I support all mandasi women, all market women in Malawi, and all tomato women in the country, that is my constituency.

In December 2010, Joyce was removed from her position in the ruling D.P.P., a decision approved by President Bingu wa Mutharika. Newspapers reported that she had been dismissed for offenses against the party, with suggestions that she encouraged Catholic Bishops to voice their disapproval of harmful government policies and planned with the President of Mozambique, Armando Guebuza, to halt President Bingu wa Mutharika's Zambezi waterway project. However, no evidence was provided to substantiate these claims. In addition, the D.P.P. used its influence over nationally owned newspapers to black Joyce out of media coverage and promote Peter Mutharika as the next presidential candidate.

Joyce decided to register a new political party with encouragement from colleagues disappointed with the D.P.P., even though the ruling party had warned her against doing so. Joyce established the People's Party (P.P.) in 2011 as threats against her well-being increased. A truck ran into her convoy and smashed into her vehicle. It so happened that a last-minute change to her plans placed her in another vehicle, and she was unhurt by the assassination attempt. She also survived another threat to her life where her security detail was stabbed to death trying to protect her. Joyce increased her criticism of the government's poor management of the economy. There were widespread protests with demands for President Bingu wa Mutharika to step down in 2011. The police response included the use of live ammunition, causing the death of several protestors. Joyce condemned the government's actions as it had allowed the use of deadly force by the police.

As Joyce continued to resist President Bingu wa Mutharika and the ruling D.P.P., he became more desperate. President Bingu wa Mutharika had to ensure that his brother Peter Mutharika succeeded him at all costs. President Bingu wa Mutharika reshuffled his Cabinet in September 2011 and left Vice President Joyce Banda off the list. He also removed nine senior and ten deputy ministers. He created a role for his wife, Callista Mutharika, as a Cabinet member with a substantial salary, placing her third in rank after Joyce. He promoted his brother Peter Mutharika to a more prominent position as Minister for Foreign Affairs. President Bingu wa Mutharika expected that after being pushed out of the Cabinet, Joyce would resign of her own free will. That was not going to happen, and in response to questions from the media regarding what she thought of President Bingu wa Mutharika's actions, Joyce said, "I'm not surprised, but I'm not moved." The Constitution of Malawi secured her place in the Cabinet. Joyce called on Malawians to press Parliament for her impeachment if the government could prove any wrongdoing on her part.

Joyce received more pressure from D.P.P. officials to vacate her position as Vice President of Malawi, with a D.P.P. spokesperson making a public call for Joyce to step down. President Bingu wa Mutharika tried to confiscate Joyce's official vehicles and cell phones and dismissed her staff. The courts blocked the removal of her security vehicles and rejected President Bingu wa Mutharika's attempt to dismiss her from office, as it was contrary to the Malawian Constitution. With no room for her within President Bingu wa Mutharika's administration, Joyce remained at home, campaigning against corruption in government and working on women's and girls' empowerment.

Despite these attacks, Joyce's credibility rating remained strong. There were reports of mass resignations from the D.P.P. to protest the treatment of Vice President Joyce Banda. By 2012, it was clear there were factions within the D.P.P., with some former D.P.P. members backing Joyce's 2014 presidential bid as the candidate for the newly formed People's Party. Many don't know that while Joyce was dealing with these difficulties within the government, her sister Catherine was battling a serious illness. Joyce had moved Catherine in with her at the official residence in Blantyre so she could assist with her care. Sadly, Catherine would lose her battle with the illness later in 2012, but this experience allowed Joyce to put the vicious attacks from her political colleagues in perspective.

On April 5, 2012, President Bingu wa Mutharika died from a cardiac arrest in South Africa, but his aides kept this a secret while they plotted to remove Joyce and install Peter Mutharika. When these associates tried to transport the deceased president's body to a secret location, it was discovered, and news of the death traveled to Malawi on April 6. The government still had not made a public announcement of the president's death. Some Cabinet members met in secret and held a press conference at midnight, claiming the president was fine, though it had become known that he had died the previous day around noon. They added that Vice President Joyce Banda had no authority to act because she was not a member of the ruling party.

Former President Bakili Muluzi called for a restoration of constitutional order and that Vice President Joyce Banda must lead the government. When the sitting president is unable to play his role, the Malawian Constitution calls upon the Vice President of Malawi to take over. Joyce had support from the European Union and countries like the United States and United Kingdom. International observers called on the Malawian government to respect the country's constitution. The Malawi Law Society confirmed the section of the Malawian Constitution that made Joyce's ascension legal, but it was clear that the Mutharika family faction would stop at nothing to prevent Joyce's succession as president.

On April 7, 2012, South Africa confirmed President Bingu wa Mutharika's death, as his associates sought a court order preventing Joyce from becoming president. Joyce called Army Commander General Henry Odillo, who agreed to station troops at her home. Joyce, surrounded by the Army and Police Commanders, military troops, the Attorney General, and others, spoke to the journalists who had gathered. She announced ten days of mourning and plans to have the late President Bingu wa Mutharika's body returned to Malawi from South Africa. Those judges, Cabinet members, and parliamentarians who had gathered at Peter Mutharika's house waiting for the court order to swear him in as president began to panic. Some left and showed up at Joyce's residence. They could be charged with treason since the objective to secure a court order had failed.

Joyce prevailed, and later in the day, on April 7, she was sworn in as the first woman President of Malawi. Joyce took her oath of office on the podium at the Parliament Building in Lilongwe. President Joyce Banda called for calm and dismissed the need for revenge against those who had made it impossible for her to carry out her previous role as Vice President of Malawi. In her speech, she expressed her hope for a peaceful transition and asked for a two-minute silence in honor of the fallen former President Bingu wa Mutharika.

I want all of us to move into the future with hope and with the spirit of oneness and unity. I hope we shall stand united, and I hope that as a God-fearing nation we allow God to come before us, because if we do not do that then we have failed.

Later, the *Guardian* newspaper in Pretoria, South Africa, interviewed Joyce. The reporter wanted to know her thoughts regarding being the first woman president in southern Africa. Joyce did not forget her cause as a grassroots activist, calling for all women to come together to help one another succeed.

It's heavy for me. I feel that I'm carrying this heavy load on behalf of all women. If I fail, I will have failed all the women in the region. But for me to succeed, they must all rally around.

Joyce began a two-year term at the Kamuzu Palace in Lilongwe. There were many across Africa who were pleased that the continent had gained its second woman president. The Maendeleo ya Wanawake Organization of Kenya awarded President Joyce Banda the *Jubilee Certificate of Honor* in November 2012. One of the women who had inspired Joyce many years previously, former Maendeleo ya Wanawake Chairperson Jane Kaino, expressed how proud she was of President Joyce Banda and her decades-long struggle for African women and girls. Almost forty years earlier, Joyce had gone to Kenya without knowing the awakening that lay in store for her.

The new President of Malawi did not forget to pay tribute to her father, Gray Mtila, who had been instrumental in the fulfillment of her destiny. Joyce walked to the balcony and looked down, just as she had watched Governor Sir Glyn Smallwood Jones do those many years ago. She remembered her father's encouraging words, "Joyce, you have the potential to go anywhere." Gray had taken his eldest daughter to the old Government House to spark her imagination, and some fifty years later, Joyce took office as the head of the nation. Wherever Uncle John was, he certainly said to himself, "I told you so, Gray."

In 2013, some eighteen months after Joyce became President of Malawi, the former President of South Africa, Nelson Mandela, passed away. Joyce traveled to South Africa for the funeral and received a rousing applause for her tribute in memory of Nelson Mandela. As a mark of her respect, President Joyce Banda talked about Nelson Mandela's influence on her leadership style, noting traits like humility and forgiveness. Joyce's memorable speech at the event described in moving terms, how she transitioned from being the vilified Vice President of Malawi to the unifying President of Malawi.

> At the moment I became President of Malawi, I had been isolated, humiliated, called names, and had an assassination attempt on my life. I found myself in a situation where I had to work with those same people that had prevented me from becoming president of my country. I had to forgive, but I had to forgive without any effort, because my Madiba had prepared me. Tata's [Nelson Mandela's] courage, determination, love, and passion for his people inspired me on my journey to becoming the first woman president of this region. I learned that leadership is about falling in love with the people that you serve and the people falling in love with you. It is about serving the people with selflessness, with sacrifice and with the need to put the common good ahead of personal interests. I am saying all this because the day after Madiba passed away, the BBC called Malawi to interview me, and they said a lot of African leaders are talking about the lessons that you ought to learn from Madiba. But are you practicing them? Are you doing it? And I said, "Yes, come and see."

When I took over, the economy had almost collapsed. I told Malawians we needed to pass through difficult times. I even cut my own salary by thirty percent to show we were making sacrifices.

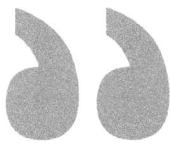

Presidential Initiatives

Chapter XII

Joyce came to head Malawi's national government at a time of great difficulty. A constitutional crisis that involved her previous position as vice president had just ended. There were allegations of government corruption, severe economic hardship with fuel shortages and high food prices, and strained international relationships. The situation was so bad that Zambia donated 1,320 gallons of gasoline to enable the government to conduct the state funeral for former President Bingu wa Mutharika.

Malawian presidents are elected for a five-year term; the late President Bingu wa Mutharika served three years, leaving Joyce with two years to make an impact on the dire conditions. Three weeks after she was sworn in as president, Joyce assumed several roles to facilitate the rebuilding tasks ahead and appointed her Cabinet of twenty-three ministers and nine deputies. She removed Peter Mutharika from his position as foreign minister and other Mutharika family supporters who had tried to bypass Malawi's Constitution after former President Bingu wa Mutharika's death, including the police chief implicated in the death of a student activist during the 2011 protests.

President Joyce Banda fixed damaged relationships with neighbors Mozambique and Botswana. She talked with the President of Zambia, Michael Sata, on a way forward for the two nations. Joyce negotiated an agreement with President Jakaya Kikwete of Tanzania, ending the conflict between the two countries. Joyce went against the African Union, refusing to host the July 2012 African Union Summit to demonstrate her opposition to a demand from the African Union. Former Sudanese Head of State Omar al-Bashir, faced with a warrant for his arrest from the International Criminal Court, sought refuge in Malawi. The African Union opposed the international court's decision, and members pressed Joyce for a confirmation that she would not enforce the warrant. For Joyce, it was not in Malawi's interest to protect someone who had an open arrest warrant from the international court. At the time, Omar al-Bashir was facing charges for war crimes.

Many countries, including the United States, Britain, Norway, and Germany, and organizations like the World Bank and African Development Bank, had ended assistance to Malawi. They had expressed disapproval of President Bingu wa Mutharika's attacks on democratic systems. This created economic difficulties for Malawi because it depended on its foreign relationships. Joyce opened conversations with the United Kingdom Foreign Office, which agreed to send a country representative on her assurances that the disrespect showed to the last British High Commissioner would not be repeated. President Bingu wa Mutharika had expelled the British High Commissioner when he criticized damaging government policies. She spoke with the United States Secretary of State, reopening talks on a possible energy grant. Joyce reached out to the European Union Foreign Affairs Office and the International Monetary Fund (IMF) Representative for Malawi.

To address electricity supply difficulties and constant power outages, the Kapichira Hydroelectric Power Station Phase II and Kam'mwamba Coal-Fired Power Plant were commissioned. Twenty-seven rural trading centers received electricity through the Malawi Rural Electrification Program. The rampant electricity cuts that were common significantly reduced when Joyce was president. Regarding fuel problems, the government increased national reserves by implementing a strategic fuel program. The groundbreaking ceremony occurred on February 18, 2014, at Mzuzu.

In the years leading up to Joyce's presidency, there was a shortage of foreign currency needed for importing essential supplies and other goods. Donors cut aid due to disagreements with the previous government, and demand for Malawi's main export, tobacco, fell. During discussions with IMF, it was recommended that the national currency, the Malawian Kwacha,

be devalued as part of the effort to attract funding for development projects. This was a difficult decision for Joyce to make because of the immediate impact on food prices and other costs of living increases. However, Joyce looked at countries like Ghana and the Seychelles, which had taken the same route and made a success of it. In May 2012, President Joyce Banda devalued the Malawian Kwacha by thirty-three percent. The devaluation led to panic buying as people feared there would be a huge price increase in goods. Shops ran out of basic supplies such as sugar, oil, and flour. By January 2013, Malawians went on extensive protests, but Joyce argued that the devaluation was necessary, caused by the previous administration's weak leadership. President Joyce Banda called for everyone to remain calm. The devaluation would increase Malawi's supply of foreign currency and the prices of exports. For example, the devaluation was beneficial to tobacco farmers. Two pounds of tobacco sold at $0.50 before the devaluation, but within a week of the change, the same quantity sold for $2.00.

The country had not seen any significant job growth during the previous ten years, increasing the percentage of Malawians living in poverty. To show how dedicated she was to improving employment opportunities, President Joyce Banda donated thirty percent of her salary to the Malawi Council for the Handicapped (MACOHA). MACOHA assists people living with disabilities acquire vocational training to make them self-sufficient. During President's Kamuzu Banda's era, he had appointed Joyce to the board and so she understood the agency's needs. Joyce's government developed the Malawi Decent Work Country Program to examine poor job growth and identify solutions. An aspect of this was the Youth Job Creation Initiative, which focused on building youth skills and creating job opportunities. This review of job growth trends led to an upgrade of the pension system with the passage of the Pension Bill. The new Pension Act mandated employers to create retirement plans for employees.

She continued with her push to increase women in national-level decision-making. Joyce assigned qualified women to vacant positions. For example, Joyce appointed the first woman governor of the Reserve Bank, who had served as deputy for many years. She appointed three women high court judges, a woman solicitor general, a woman deputy inspector of police, a woman director of the civil service, eighteen women permanent secretaries, and other women directors of government departments. She appointed men and women under the age of forty years to encourage the generation of fresh ideas. Joyce reexamined the child labor issues she had faced as Minister for Gender, Child Welfare, and Community Services. Her government developed a plan to end child labor, and in September 2012, the national conference on the problem highlighted strategies for eliminating the practice.

Joyce signed a new flag bill into law, boosting her popularity. In 2010, then President Bingu wa Mutharika changed the rising sun flag adopted at independence on the grounds that Malawi was no longer a developing nation and must be represented by a full sun. The new flag was unpopular because it seemed like an attempt to rewrite national history, erasing the connection between the rising sun and the independence struggle. There were many protests during the transition, which President Bingu wa Mutharika ignored. In May 2012, Joyce led the vote in Parliament to readopt the rising sun flag, with collaboration from all opposition members except those in the D.P.P.

After the birth of her fourth child, Joyce experienced a serious complication that put her life at risk. As a result, she personally identified with the struggle that pregnant women faced. Joyce continued with her crusade to improve maternal and child health by launching the Presidential Initiative on Maternal Health and Safe Motherhood. In African communities, chiefs are influential and trusted leaders. Joyce tapped into this resource to assist with the struggle to reduce maternal deaths in Malawi within a week of her inauguration. She called two hundred and fifty chiefs to a meeting at the Mount Soche Hotel in Blantyre, recruiting them as partners in a government initiative. This was a unique program where chiefs were participating in a national discussion at the local level.

The chiefs agreed with the objective of decreasing maternal deaths through healthy pregnancies and births. The leaders organized themselves into a national committee chaired by Senior Chief Kwataine, who received a vehicle for traveling around the country recruiting partners and sharing strategies. This was a novel idea in Malawi, where men directly discussed family planning, safe pregnancies, and births in a public forum. The senior chief spoke on television and radio about the health benefits of having fewer children, and on how responsible men cared for their wives during pregnancies and took them to hospitals or clinics for safe deliveries. The role the senior chief played grew so prominent that he spoke at an African Union meeting and the United Nations in New York, United States.

Through Senior Chief Kwataine's campaign, other traditional leaders were encouraged to follow his lead. Some chiefs passed local ordinances where women were not allowed to have babies in the village attended by traditional birthing assistants but in clinics or hospitals. If a woman died during childbirth, the chief would be held responsible, having to pay a fine to his senior chief. Non-compliant women and birthing assistants also paid fines. Traditional birthing assistants were transformed into *Secret Mothers*, helping women have healthy pregnancies and accompanying pregnant women to clinics or hospitals when their due time arrived. There was soon a competition among chiefs for the community with the lowest maternal death count.

The initiative's success stemmed from the effective collaboration between chiefs, husbands of pregnant women, traditional birthing assistants, pregnant women, and other women and men in the village, all supporting healthy pregnancies and deliveries. Through this national committee on maternal health, chiefs and community residents formed other national committees on nutrition and girls' education. Joyce's sister-friend Chrissie had a prominent role on the education committee. Chief Kwataine became a hero when deaths during pregnancy and childbirth were eliminated in all eighty-nine villages within his jurisdiction. Kwataine had a prior two decades' worth of experience, showing that this issue could be addressed from a local level. He created a local registry of pregnant women, with outcomes reported to the village chief, making the village chief responsible. In addition to punishment for those who breached the rules, he rewarded those who enforced the rules, protecting the lives of mothers and babies.

The maternal health initiative included the construction of twenty holding shelters with funding from the private sector. While pregnant women waited for their due dates, they were housed in these shelters, located close to delivery clinics or hospitals. Pregnant women some-

times traveled long distances to clinics or hospitals, often during the onset of labor. There were fewer maternal deaths if pregnant women traveled before going into labor and waited at a shelter. Within two years, Joyce's Presidential Initiative led to reduced maternal mortality ratios, from 675 deaths for every 100,000 live births to 460 deaths for every 100,000 live births, a reduction of thirty percent.

Joyce assembled a team to investigate government corruption when she was informed by the European Union Ambassador to Malawi that the financial management system was being abused. She sought funding from the British government for a financial review. A contract was signed with Baker Tilly, the international auditing company recommended by the British government. Joyce's determination to stamp out government corruption reached a new height when an assassination attempt was made on Paul Mphwiyo as he returned to his Lilongwe home on September 13, 2013. He was the budget director at the Ministry of Finance, appointed by Joyce to investigate rumors of official mishandling of public money. After the shooting, Joyce issued a statement indicating that it was a deliberate attempt to stop inquiries into public sector corruption.

Investigations into the assassination attempt exposed what came to be known as *Cashgate* or the *Cashgate Scandal*, where senior government members were alleged to have stolen an estimated $32 million. It emerged that public servants collaborated with the private sector to milk the government through contracts. At the start, ten government officials were arrested on suspicion of being part of the corruption ring. On October 10, 2013, after Joyce returned from the United Nations in New York, she dismissed her Cabinet because it had been revealed that several members had participated in Cashgate. Joyce established a commission of police and government officials to conduct a financial audit across all public service departments. On October 15, 2013, she appointed a new Cabinet with two noticeable absences. Finance Minister Ken Lipenga and Justice Minister Ralph Kasambara did not return to their positions.

Joyce provided updates on the review's progress, cooperating with investigators and accepting responsibility, as the scandal broke while she was president. Over sixty individuals were arrested in connection with Cashgate, with some being found guilty and sentenced to imprisonment. Despite these efforts to restore confidence in government financial dealings, Joyce's reputation took a severe beating with negative media coverage.

When Joyce left the presidency in 2014, her government programs had achieved success in many areas. The Joyce Banda administration increased the availability of fuel supplies from seven to fifteen days, with reserves under construction. The recovery plan grew the country's economy from 1.8% in 2012 to 6.2% in 2014. Maternal health initiatives improved outcomes, saving the lives of mothers and their newborns. Food stores multiplied with bountiful maize harvests. With a stable Malawian Kwacha, the availability of foreign currency for the importation of essential items increased. Before Joyce took over, foreign currency availability covered only one week; it grew to three and a half months during her term. The supply of electricity improved, and twenty-seven rural areas received electricity. Joyce strengthened democratic processes by removing restrictions on civil liberties and press freedom and signed a new bill that mandated government officials to declare assets annually.

> My mission in life is to assist women with social and political empowerment through business and education.

Life After Politics

Joyce Banda stood as the People's Party (P.P.) presidential candidate in the 2014 general elections, winning twenty percent of the vote, coming third in a slate of twelve candidates. Peter Mutharika of the Democratic Progress Party (D.P.P.) was declared the winner with thirty-six percent of the vote. Many commentators noted that Cashgate overshadowed Joyce's two-year governmental successes. The new D.P.P. government embarked on a campaign to discredit Joyce. It seemed that just as the late President Bingu wa Mutharika had harassed his predecessor with arrest warrants, President Peter Mutharika planned to subject Joyce to the same treatment. For the safety of herself and her family, Joyce decided to live outside Malawi for a few years. After all, if she could secure an international platform, she could continue as an advocate for women's and girls' rights.

After Joyce left Malawi, she received fellowships at the Center for Global Development and the Woodrow Wilson Center in Washington, D.C. In addition, she served on various international boards, such as the Executive Advisory Committee of UNIFEM (United Nations Development Fund for Women) and Scientific Advisory Board for Global Health and Social Change at the Harvard Medical School. She became a member of the Council of Women World Leaders, an organization of former women prime ministers, presidents, and other heads of government endorsing women in high political office. It was created by the first woman president of Iceland, who was also the first woman in the world, elected through a democratic system to the office of president. In 2017, Joyce was one of the founding members of the African Women Leaders Network, a group of over three hundred African women leaders collaborating to develop other women leaders.

Joyce traveled extensively, lecturing on women's and girls' empowerment and writing research papers. She shared her experiences from her advocacy and as a woman in political leadership in Africa. In 2018, she published *From Day One: Why Supporting Girls Aged 0 to 10 is Critical to Change Africa's Path* through the Center for Global Development, with the assistance of Caroline Lambert. The book was based on an earlier paper published in 2016, *An Agenda for Harmful Cultural Practices and Girls' Empowerment*. The book discusses the importance of reaching girls aged zero to ten years, critical years where young minds are trained on what to expect in life. It provides the rationale for Joyce's dedication to grassroots activism and outlines factors such as poor nutrition, abuse, the burden of work, and lack of education, that prevent girls from reaching their full potential as women. The book identifies data collection, legal reform, and change of negative mindsets as solutions to the problems highlighted.

After three years in the United States, Joyce decided to return to Malawi. Joyce informed Peter Mutharika's government of her plans in July 2017 and a warrant for her arrest was announced the following week. It accused her of abusing her position and money laundering during her two years as president. Joyce denied the charges of wrongdoing, knowing it was a backlash from her crusade against public sector corruption during her time in government. In January 2018, Malawi's Anti-Corruption Bureau announced it found no evidence against Joyce. It looked like a calculated effort by her detractors simply to attack her credibility. The independent audit Joyce had ordered with British government funding by Baker Tilly reported its findings in 2014. The publicly available report did not find links between Joyce and any corrupt activities. In addition, the National Audit Office did not find any connection between Joyce and Cashgate.

In April 2018, Joyce made travel reservations for her trip to Malawi, prepared to confront attacks from the government and possible arrest for corruption. There had been no public announcement from the police noting that charges had been dropped after the Anti-Corruption Bureau's report. Joyce traveled through South Africa, where she gave an interview to Reuters. She confirmed she was returning home because she was not guilty of any wrongdoing. She was the only president to date who had appointed a commission of inquiry into corruption by public officials during her tenure.

The plane carrying Joyce landed at Malawi's Chileka International Airport where there was a crowd of supporters packed at the arrival gate while others forced their way onto the tarmac. The arrest warrant was not enforced, and no charges were filed. She declared her intention to stand as a presidential candidate in the 2019 general elections if she secured the P.P.'s chairperson position. Joyce launched a political campaign, attending over twelve rallies and meetings across the country between her arrival in April and June 2018. By September, Joyce had won the P.P.'s presidential candidate nomination with ninety-seven percent of the vote. Within the next few months, the landscape became crowded with twenty presidential hopefuls. There was no way the sitting President Peter Mutharika of the D.P.P. would be defeated with such a large pool of candidates. Joyce began to host meetings with the different political parties for a strong coalition to defeat the D.P.P.'s candidate.

In March 2019, Joyce withdrew her candidacy after a long meeting with the P.P.'s National Executive Committee. She backed Lazarus Chakwera, candidate of the Malawi Congress Party (M.C.P.), the second largest political party. The P.P. and M.C.P. released a joint statement confirming the collaboration, putting early predictions of Peter Mutharika's success on shaky ground. "Malawi is bigger than individuals," the joint P.P. and M.C.P. statement noted. "As such, we all have set aside individual aspirations and embrace the greater and common good." With Joyce's endorsement, Lazarus Chakwera had a good chance of victory. Peter Mutharika had exceeded Lazarus Chakwera by only 400,000 votes in the 2014 general elections.

During the May 2019 elections, Peter Mutharika emerged with 38.6% of the vote to Lazarus Chakwera's 35.4%. The elections were declared invalid by the High Court, confirmed by the Supreme Court, on the grounds of widespread voting irregularities. The re-run elections were held in June 2020, and Lazarus Chakwera, with 59.3% of the vote, defeated Peter Mutharika. Joyce kept a busy campaign schedule. After the 2020 elections, she returned to her role as a community activist and at the Joyce Banda Foundation and speaking at international meetings while working on the many boards she chaired or served as a member.

Malawians must look forward toward a better future.

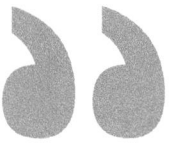

The Joyce Effect

Chapter XIV

Does Her Excellency Mrs. Joyce Banda live up to her name? Did Grandmother Hilda's decision to give a voice to her granddaughter's destiny all those years ago at the clinic in Domasi light the path ahead of Baby Joyce? Grandmother Hilda hoped that her new granddaughter would emulate the worthy traits she identified in Nurse Joyce. Did Baby Joyce grow up to nurture authority and use it to bring new life? Did Baby Joyce grow up to create joy in the lives she touched?

Well, first, the foundation for Joyce's life had to be laid. Through her relationship with Father Gray and Mother Edith and family life in Zomba and Malemia, Joyce acquired critical training. She learned to shoulder the heavy burden of responsibility, developed the ability to dream, and recognized that hard work made dreams a reality. When childhood friend Chrissie was forced to drop out of school, Joyce made a commitment to herself. There was a harsh lesson for Joyce as a woman in an abusive relationship with young children to protect, not knowing where the next meal would come from if she walked out of the bad relationship. It was an experience that widened the group of people she hoped to assist in the future. The life-threatening health condition that she endured after the birth of her fourth child, again, added a new focus. The help with her destiny she found in her beloved husband, retired Chief Justice Richard Banda. Then, most important of all, the mercy and grace of God being the glue that made it all come together for good. For Joyce, her relationship with God is the cornerstone of her life. Joyce confirmed in her 2018 Landon Lecture at Kansas State University in the United States that the difficulties she had experienced in life informed the choices she made.

I have been fortunate that all the things that I have championed in my life have come directly from my personal experiences. Each of us has our own story that shapes us, and it is our individual responsibility to contribute to the common good and positively impact lives worldwide.

Joyce's start to bringing new life and creating joy came from the financial independence she gained as a successful entrepreneur. Before establishing the National Association of Business Women (NABW), on a much smaller scale, she gave classes on the basics of running a business. She demonstrated to the women the sense of freedom and exhilaration associated with having some degree of economic security. Joyce taught these women that they did not have to live in hopelessness, feeling trapped in their circumstances because there was hope.

Then came the NABW, a more structured approach to her early lectures; an organization that still assists thousands of women and their children out of desperate poverty. The Joyce Banda Foundation (JBF), established after the NABW, that has reached over one million people, providing access to education, promoting businesses owned by women, and training the youth. The bright green signature cloth of JBF's Market Women Activities Initiative (MWAI) is a symbol of possibilities and unity for participating women. Joyce transitioned to the political sphere, where she continued to champion women's and girls' rights. She created the dramatic foundation for the protection of women against domestic violence and designed presidential initiatives that saved the lives of mothers and their newborn babies through safe birthing practices.

Joyce's pathway was not easy. For example, as the Vice President of Malawi, opponents tried to demean her work as an activist, where she had enhanced the lives of Malawians through different entities she established. There were attempts at public humiliation with her dismissal from national organizations and the ruling political party. Joyce endured death threats and assassination attempts. She stood her ground though pressed on all sides to accept Peter Mutharika as successor to his brother, the late President Bingu wa Mutharika. However, when she became President of Malawi, she chose reconciliation instead of retaliation because she knew that was what her country needed.

As President Joyce Banda, she recognized that structures for development projects were failing, but she found ways around it. She often described herself as a "hitchhiker." Joyce formed a partnership with local rulers to improve maternal health outcomes. Joyce fought against corruption in public office, even though she knew that it might backfire, causing her to lose the 2014 elections, which it did. She led the way by commissioning the first government audit that provided evidence against public officials engaged in corrupt activities, leading to criminal charges and imprisonments. There were loud conversations accusing her of being a part of the problem, but the independent audit report released in 2014 helped to establish her innocence. After the 2014 elections, she understood that for the safety of her family and herself, she must live outside her beloved Malawi due to persecution from the Peter Mutharika administration. All the adversity failed to shift Joyce's emphasis, becoming a fellow at two institutions in the United States, where she had a platform for her activism for women and girls.

Today, Joyce does not rest. She travels widely, speaking at international meetings, including the United Nations world conferences on women, Harvard Kennedy School, London School of Economics and Political Science, and African Women's Forum. Joyce increases awareness of the challenges faced by women and girls, works with groups for better outcomes for women, girls, and the youth, and expands existing programs that uplift women to include men. Just a few months ago, she was in Addis Ababa speaking at the Harvard Ministers' Leadership Round Table, organized by Harvard University each year, to allow former presidents to share experiences with those serving as government ministers.

Joyce remains active on many boards. Since 2015, Joyce has served as the chairperson for the International Sheroes Forum, a wing of the Sheroes Foundation headquartered in Ghana. Sheroes pushes women's and girls' social and economic advancement in Africa. The Sheroes Elect Her Initiative partners with the Joyce Banda Foundation to support women seeking political leadership. The International Sheroes Foundation launched the *Joyce Banda Political Leadership Award* in 2018; its first recipient was Dr. Bibi Ameenah Gurib-Fakim, President of Mauritius, from 2015-2018. Joyce has served on Nutrition International's board since 2016. This Canada-based organization tackles malnutrition across the world. In 2022, Joyce was appointed honorary chair of the *Women Empowerment and Development Society in Asia-Africa* for her "outstanding achievement in the field of women development, capacity building, and corporation." Other boards where she lends her expertise include the Tana Forum focused on security issues in Africa and the African Union Committee of Elders, composed of serving and past female heads of state.

Through the Joyce Banda Foundation, Joyce continues advocacy for women's and girls' rights and development. In 2015, she founded the Joyce Banda Africa Initiative to push women to strive for positions in leadership. The Joyce Banda Africa Initiative partners with other organizations to promote women in political leadership. The first week of each month, Joyce visits a JBF Orphan Care center to assess program outcomes and offer support to staff. Joyce believes that to empower women to build better lives for themselves and their families, the girl child must be reached before she becomes a teenager. During these years, change will have the most significant impact. However, JBF works with all age groups. For the 2022 International Day of the Girl Child, for example, JBF partnered with Plan International to hold a meeting for young women between the ages of sixteen and eighteen years. This forum discussed problems that young women faced and how these may be addressed.

As she did in the past, Joyce combines this busy schedule with a full family life. She is committed to her husband of many decades, Richard. She describes him as her best friend and partner in all that she does. Someone who stands by her, celebrating her victories and encouraging her during difficult moments. As they grow old together, Joyce and Richard enjoy Alan Jackson's song, *I Want to Stroll over Heaven with You*. Joyce is a mother and grandmother of her biological and many adopted children, of her community, and her nation. In February 2021, Joyce dealt with the death of her son Geoffrey from the COVID-19 disease, always wearing the title *amayi* (or mother) with grace despite challenges, whether within her family or nation.

Joyce certainly lives up to Grandmother Hilda's expectations. She "delivers" life like Nurse Joyce, helping women and girls build better futures for themselves. She brings joy; many countless people have benefitted from the programs she originated. She enables women and girls to dream of possibilities and makes aspirations a reality. Just as Nurse Joyce's midwife specialization meant that her clients were girls in their youth and women, so does Joyce's focus remain on girls and women. Like Grandmother Hilda, now Grandmother Joyce had the privilege of naming a beautiful granddaughter in July 2018. She gave the name *Nginawe Kutujaliwa Ambuje*, (i.e., Our Heavenly Father will continue to bless us. He has only started.) Grandmother Joyce expects Nginawe to be a blessing to all who come her way.

There is no doubt that Joyce has changed the lives of many Malawians. When she returned home in 2018, there were hundreds of people at the airport waiting to welcome her. Many were dressed in the People's Party color of orange, singing and dancing on the streets of Blantyre all the way to Domasi. Amayi had returned home! Yes, her critics may have many things to say, but her compassion for humanity shows through her national and international work. Joyce's dedication and perseverance to her country make her an inspiration to many.

Despite all her achievements, Her Excellency Mrs. Joyce Banda remains humble. When she appeared on the Times Square Billboard again in 2022, she expressed gratitude to God, believing that obedience to God and service to God's people brings its own reward and recognition. In her words, "God's favor falls upon you in ways beyond your imagination."

Joyce, the value of a name given with hope, promise, and expectation. Tradition quite rightly had to stop to ensure that Joyce got what she needed when her life started, and along the way, to guide her towards fulfilling her destiny.

Joyce's Leadership Nuggets

Appendix A

#1

Leadership is a love affair. You must fall in love with the people you serve, and the people must fall in love with you. Then you have political capital.

This restrains a leader from acting in a way that is not advantageous to the people served. A leader must be prepared to stay the course, refuse temptation, and make the interests of the people served a priority.

#2

As a woman leader you must be resilient, and you must be determined to take risks.

A leader must realize that he or she is in service to the people and must be accountable. A leader must engage the people in the decision-making process. A leader must be prepared to take risks and maintain links at the grassroots level.

#3

I have been extremely lucky to be the one that implemented issues that emerged from personal experience, namely education, maternal health, income into poor households, and human rights.

The definition of leadership has changed over the years. A leader must always bear in mind that influential groups can emerge from all areas. For example, women in the marketplace or people motivated by a particular personal experience or need may grow into a powerful force. These groups must be given a platform and allowed to contribute to the narrative.

Accolades

2011:
- The 3rd Most Powerful Woman in Africa (Forbes)

2012:
- Malawi's 4th President
- Malawi's 1st Woman President
- Malawi's 2nd Woman Head of State (after Queen Elizabeth II)
- Africa's 2nd Woman President (after Liberia's Ellen Johnson Sirleaf)
- Malawi's 1st Woman Vice President
- One of Africa's Most Influential People (New African Magazine, Britain)
- Africa's Most Powerful Woman (Forbes)
- The 71st Most Powerful Woman in the World (Forbes)

2013:
- Africa's Most Powerful Woman (Forbes)
- One of the World's Most Powerful Black Women (Forbes)
- The 47th Most Powerful Woman in the World (Forbes)

2014:
- The 40th Most Powerful Woman in the World (Forbes)
- The Most Powerful Woman in Africa (Forbes)
- The BBC's 100 Women (BBC)

- One of the World's Most Powerful Black Women (Forbes)
- One of the 100 Most Influential People in the World (Time)
- One of the 100 Most Influential People in the World (Forbes)
- One of the Most Inspirational Women in Politics (CNN)
- Leading Woman of the Year in Politics (CNN)

2016:
- One of the 12 Most Powerful and Influential Women Politicians in Africa (African Leadership Magazine)

Awards

1997:
- Africa Prize for Leadership for the Sustainable End of Hunger (Hunger Project, New York, U.S.A.)
- Woman of the Year (Nation Publications Limited, Malawi)

1998:
- International Award for Entrepreneurship Development (African Federation of Woman Entrepreneurs and Economic Commission for Africa)
- Woman of the Year (Nation Publications Limited, Malawi)
- 100 Heroines Award (Rochester, New York)

2001:
- Certificate of Honors (Federation of World Peace and Love, Taiwan)

2005:
- Role Models of Excellence (Government/Civil Society Leadership Award, American and African Business Women's Alliance, Washington, D.C., U.S.A.)

2006:
- Rita E. Hauser Award (Rita E. Hauser, New York, U.S.A.)
- International Award for the Health and Dignity of Women (Americans for United Nations Population Fund)

2010:
- Person of the Year (Nyasa Times Multimedia, Malawi)
- Women of Substance Award (Special Recognition Category, African Women Development Fund)

2012:
- Rev. Dr. Martin Luther King Drum Major for Freedom Award (National Press Club, Washington, D.C., U.S.A.)
- Legend Award for Leadership (African Methodist Episcopal Church of Greater Mount Nebo, Washington, D.C., U.S.A.)
- Africa's Most Inspirational Female Leader of the Year (Centre for Economic and Leadership Development, New York, U.S.A.)
- Jubilee Certificate of Honour (Maendeleo Ya Wanawake, Kenya)

2013:
- Honorary Doctorate (Jeonju University, South Korea)

2015:
- Living Legends Award (African Union)
- Legacy Award (International Women's Forum)
- Women of Distinction Global Leadership Award in Politics (Celebrating Women International)
- Honorary Doctorate (Wheelock College, Boston, Massachusetts, U.S.A.)

2016:
- GC4W Global Women Champion (International Women's Day Awards Gala, Global Connections for Women Foundation)
- A Woman of Distinction (Professional Women's Network, Malawi)

2020:
- Women Political Leaders Trailblazer Award (Reykjavík Global Forum – Women Leaders 2020)

2021:
- Honorary Doctorate (Colgate University, Hamilton, New York, U.S.A.)

2022:
- Certificate of Recognition Award as an "Inter-generational Development Champion" (National Planning Commission, Malawi)

2023:
- Women of Substance Award (Pan African Learning and Growth Network, Women in Management and Leadership, and Plan International)

References

Banda, Joyce. Joyce Banda Facebook Posts from 29 November 2022 – 15 January 2018. *Facebook*, 29 November 2022, https://www.facebook.com/DrJoyceBanda/.

"Former President of Malawi, Dr. Joyce Banda Named Honorary Chair of Women Empowerment and Development Society in Asia-Africa." *African Leadership Magazine*, 2 September 2022, https://www.africanleadershipmagazine.co.uk/former-president-of-malawi-dr-joyce-banda-named-honorary-chair-of-women-empowerment-development-society-asia-africa. Accessed 1 December 2022.

"Ex-President Banda Pulls Out of Malawi Presidential Race." *Reuters*, 14 March 2019, https://www.reuters.com/article/us-malawi-election/ex-president-banda-pulls-out-of-malawi-presidential-race-idUSKCN1QV2R3. Accessed 9 November 2022.

Banda, Mabvuto. "Former Malawi President Joyce Banda Returns from Exile." *VOA News*, 23 April 2018, https://www.voanews.com/a/former-malawi-president-joyce-banda-returns-exile/4361271.html. Accessed 9 November 2022.

Banda, Joyce. "Landon Lecture Series on Public Issues." 29 January 2018. Landon, https://www.k-state.edu/landon/speakers/joyce-banda/transcript.htm/. Transcript.

Banda, Joyce, and Caroline Lambert. From Day One: *Why Supporting Girls Aged 0 to 10 is Critical to Change Africa's Path*. Center for Global Development, 2018.

"Malawi's Former President Says 'Innocent' of Graft, Will Return Home." *Reuters*, 1 August 2017, https://www.reuters.com/article/us-malawi-corruption/malawis-former-president-says-innocent-of-graft-will-return-home-idUSKBN1AH4NE. Accessed 9 November 2022.

"Malawi Issues Arrest Warrant for Former President Over Graft Scandal." *Reuters*, 31 July 2017, https://www.reuters.com/article/uk-malawi-corruption/malawi-issues-arrest-warrant-for-former-president-over-graft-scandal-idUKKBN1AG23X. Accessed 9 November 2022.

Chikapa, Tiyesere M. "The 'Joyce Banda Effect': Explaining the Discrepancy between Public Opinion and Voting Behavior." *Women in Politics in Malawi*, edited by I. Amundsen and H. Kayuni, Chr. Michelsen Institute, 2016, pp. 45-56.

Chikapa, Tiyesere M. "Women in Politics in Malawi: An Introduction." *Women in Politics in Malawi*, edited by I. Amundsen and H. Kayuni, Chr. Michelsen Institute, 2016, pp. 1-10.

Banda, Joyce, and Priscilla Atansah. *An Agenda for Harmful Cultural Practices and Girls' Empowerment*. Center for Global Development, 2016.

"A Conversation with Her Excellency Joyce Banda." *YouTube*, uploaded by the Institute of Politics at the Harvard Kennedy School, 16 October 2015, https://www.youtube.com/watch?v=n2OB9a2gKhA.

Dulani, Boniface and Joseph Chunga. "When is Incumbency no Longer an Advantage: Explaining President Joyce Banda's Defeat." *The Malawi 2014 Tripartite Elections: Is Democracy Maturing*, edited by N. Patel and M. Whaman, The National Initiative for Civic Education, 2015, pp. 236-257.

Kamwendo, Juliet and Gregory Kwamwendo. "When Exploitation is Camouflaged as Women Empowerment: The Case of Malawi's First Female President Joyce Banda." *Feminist Africa*, no. 20, 2015, pp. 77-81.

Zimmerman, Brigitte. "Voter Response to Scandal: Cashgate." *The Malawi 2014 Tripartite Elections: Is Democracy Maturing*, edited by N. Patel and M. Whaman, The National Initiative for Civic Education, 2015, pp. 215-235.

Banda, Joyce. "Wheelock College Commencement Address." 15 May 2015. https://awpc.cattcenter.iastate.edu/2017/03/09/wheelock-college-commencement-address-may-15-2015/. Transcript.

Somanje, Caroline. "EW's Big Interview: Joyce Banda." *MW Nation*, 21 September 2014, https://mwnation.com/ew%E2%80%99s-big-interview-joyce-banda/. Accessed 9 November 2022.

"Malawi Joyce Banda Sacks Cabinet Amid Corruption Row." *BBC*, 13 October 2013, https://www.bbc.com/news/world-africa-24484557. Accessed 9 November 2022.

Banda, Joyce. "Joyce Banda. Address at the 102nd International Labor Conference." *ILO*, June 2013, https://www.ilo.org/ilc/ILCSessions/previous-sessions/102/media-centre/speeches/WCMS_215752/lang--en/index.htm. Transcript.

Crossette, Barbara. "A Traditional Chief Slashes Maternal Deaths in Malawi." *Pass Blue*, 18 April 2013, https://www.passblue.com/2013/04/18/a-traditional-chief-slasjes-maternal-deaths-in-malawi/. Accessed 1 December 2022.

Scott, Charlotte H. "Moving Towards a Post-2015 Development Agenda – Lessons from Malawi: An Interview with Her Excellency Madam Joyce Banda, President of Malawi." *IDS Bulletin*, vol. 44, no. 5, 2013, pp. 10-13.

"Kenyan Women Honour Malawi Leader Joyce Banda." *Nyasa Times*, 28 November 2012, https://www.nyasatimes.com/kenyan-women-honour-malawi-leader-joyce-banda/. Accessed 18 January 2023.

"Call it Kamuzu Palace, JB Names Malawi New State House." *Nyasa Times*, 18 November 2012, https://www.nyasatimes.com/call-it-kamuzu-palace-jb-namex-malawi-new-state-house/. Accessed 4 April 2023.

"JB Says Won't Reverse Malawi Kwacha Devaluation: IMF Chief Defends Move." Nyasa Times, 6 January 2013, https://www.nyasatimes.com/jb-says-wont-reverse-malawi-kwacha-devaluation-imf-chief-defends-move/. Accessed 9 November 2022.

"Malawi MPs Vote to Fly Old Rising Sun Flag." *BBC*, 29 May 2012, https://www.bbc.com/news/world-africa-18255188. Accessed 9 November 2022.

"Malawi Devalues Kwacha by 33%, Leading to Panic Buying." *BBC*, 7 May 2012, https://www.bbc.com/news/world-africa-17982062. Accessed 9 November 2022.

"Joyce Banda Puts Women's Rights at Centre of New Presidency." *The Pretoria Guardian*, 29 April 2012, https://www.theguardian.com/world/2012/apr/29/malawi-president-joyce-banda-women-rights. Accessed 9 November 2022.

Sachs, Jeffrey. "How Malawi Fed Its Own People." *New York Times*, 19 April 2012, https://www.nytimes.com/2012/04/20/opinion/how-malawi-fed-its-own-people.html. Accessed 6 September 2022.

Mwagiru, Ciugu. "Malawi's Joyce Banda and the Rise of Women in African Politics." *Monitor*, 18 April 2012, http://www.monitor.co.ug/artsculture/Reviews/-/691232/1388740/-/diw45/-/. Accessed 13 December 2022.

"How Nairobi Shaped Future President." *Nation*, 13 April 2012, updated 3 July 2020, https://nation.africa/kenya/news/how-nairobi-shaped-future-president--808056. Accessed 4 September 2022.

"Malawi's Iron Lady Joyce Banda." *Nation Africa*, April 12, 2012, https://nation.africa/kenya/life-and-style/dn2/malawi-s-iron-lady-joyce-banda-807900. Accessed 13 December 2022.

"Joyce Banda Sworn in as New Malawi President." *BBC*, 12 April 2012, https://www.bbc.com/news/world-africa-17644009. Accessed 23 November 2022.

Rockefeller, Marilyn M., and Joan Johnson-Freese. "Dancing for Democracy: Understanding Malawi's First Female President." *Orbis*, vol. 57, no. 2, 2012, pp. 268-281.

"Malawi: Mutharika's Estranged Deputy 'Unmoved' by Malawi Cabinet Snub." *Afrique Jet*, 9 September 2011, http://www.afriquejet.com/malawi-cabinet-snub-2011090921991.html. Accessed 12 December 2022.

"Malawi: Vice-President's Woes Dominate Malawi Media." *Afrique Jet*, 18 December 2010, http://www.afriquejet.com/news/africa-news/malawi:-vice-president%27s-woes-dominate-malawi-media-2010121864614.html. Accessed 4 September 2022.

Jomo, Frank. "Malawi's Vice President Joyce Banda Expelled from Ruling Party." *Bloomberg News*, 13 December 2010, https://www.bloomberg.com/news/articles/2010-12-13/malawi-s-vice-president-joyce-banda-expelled-from-ruling-party. Accessed 4 September 2010.

www.ingramcontent.com/pod-product-compliance
Lightning Source LLC
Chambersburg PA
CBHW062024050526
44107CB00105B/870